GOOD FOOD, JUNK FOOD, ROTTEN FOOD

SCIENCE BOOK FOR KIDS 5-7

CHILDREN'S SCIENCE EDUCATION BOOKS

In this book, we're going to talk about which foods are good for you and which are not. So, let's get right to it!

Almost everyone loves to eat! One of the reasons we eat is because food tastes good. However, the most important reason that we need to eat is because we need energy to live and do the things we like to do. Proper eating is important so you can give your body the "fuel" it needs to function.

low fat milk
Yogurt

Both adults and kids need the right types of foods to get the nutrients they need.

Your body needs:

Vitamins

Minerals

Carbohydrates

Protein

Fat

Vitamin A is very important for the health of your eyes, skin, and immune system. Vitamin A is found in milk and eggs and also in vegetables that are orange or green in color.

min A
FOODS WITH VITAMIN A

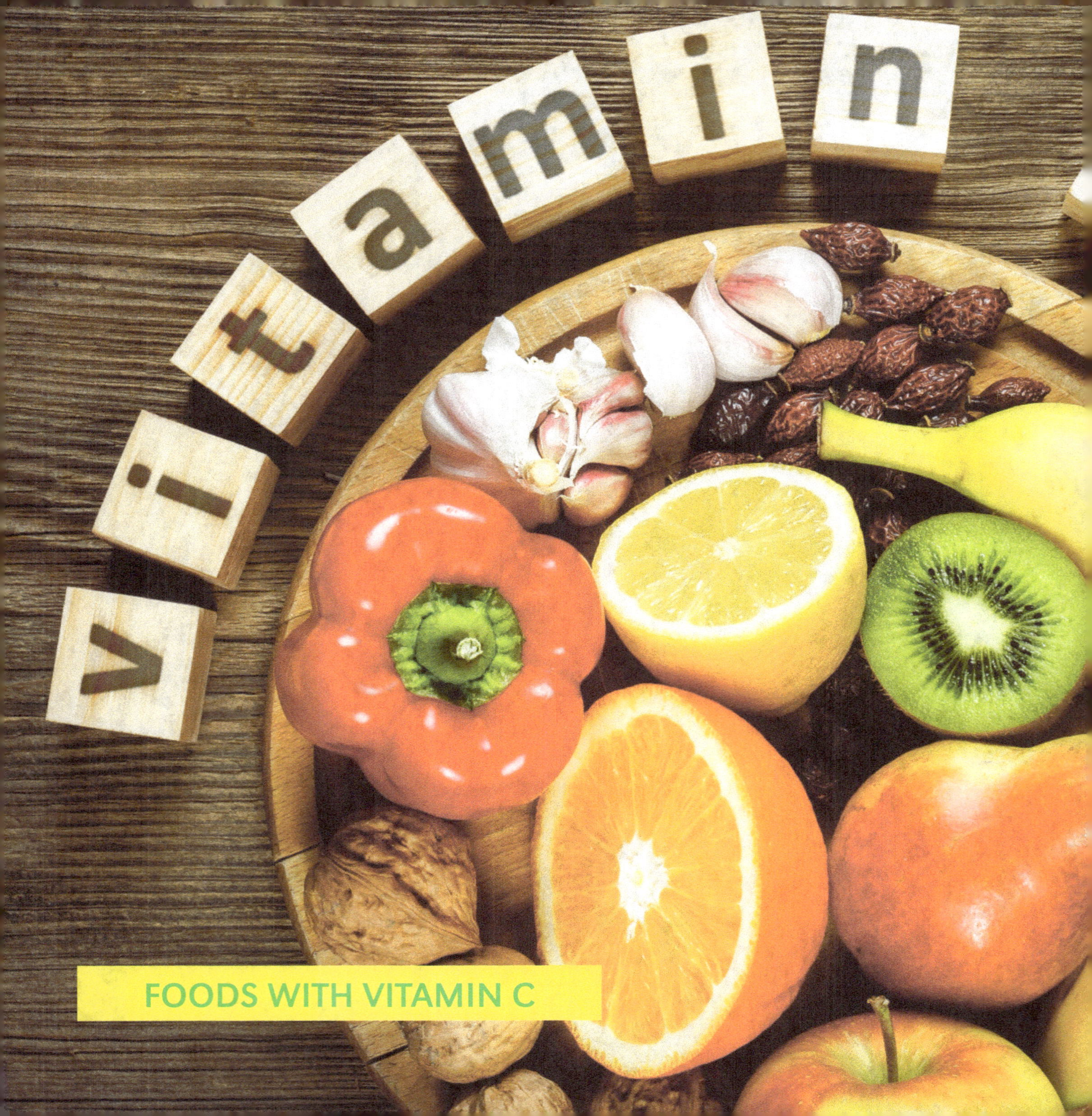

vitamin
FOODS WITH VITAMIN C

Vitamin C is critical to your bones and blood vessels. It's also important for the health of your teeth and gums. Without vitamin C, your brain wouldn't function properly either. Vitamin C is found in oranges, berries, spinach, and tomatoes.

Vitamin D is critical to your bones and can be found in milk, eggs, and fish oil. You also get Vitamin D through being out in sunlight.

n
D
FOODS WITH VITAMIN C

VITAMIN
FOODS WITH VITAMIN E

Vitamin E is needed for your blood and your cells to stay healthy. Nuts, whole grains, and green leafy vegetables all have Vitamin E.

Vitamin B12 is important for your red blood cells and Vitamin B6 is important to brain function. Both of these vitamins are important for your nervous system too.

VITAMIN
B6

VITAMIN
B12

Vitamin B12 can be found in fish, red meat, and poultry and Vitamin B6 can be found in these same foods as well as bananas, nuts, and beans.

Your body also needs thiamin, niacin, riboflavin, and folate. If you eat a healthy diet, you should be getting the vitamins you need every day. Your doctor might recommend a vitamin or mineral supplement if he or she feels you're not getting enough important nutrients from the foods you eat.

MINERALS

In addition to vitamins, our bodies need minerals. Some of the most important minerals we need are calcium, iron, magnesium, phosphorus, potassium, and zinc.

Calcium is important to your bones and your teeth. You can get enough calcium if your regular meals have servings of milk, cheese, yogurt, and green vegetables. You need iron for your red blood cells. Your meals should include red meat, poultry, fish, pork, soy, and green leafy veggies.

CALCIUM

Mg

Magnesium is important for your muscles, nerves, and bones. Nuts, breads, milk, whole grains, and bananas all contain magnesium. Milk, fish, and meat all contain phosphorus, which is important to build strong bones, teeth, and cells. Both magnesium and phosphorus are critical for your energy level.

Potassium is important for your muscles as well as your nervous system. Bananas and broccoli both contain potassium. Potatoes and other types of fruit contain potassium too. Zinc is a vital mineral for your immune system. When your body is healing an injury, it needs zinc. Zinc is contained in whole grains, poultry, nuts, and seafood.

ssium

CARBOHYDRATES

Starchy vegetables, such as potatoes, corn, and peas, all contain carbohydrates. Beans, such as kidney beans and pinto beans, contain carbohydrates. Grains like rice, barley, and oats all contain carbohydrates as well. Your body needs carbohydrates for energy. However, if you eat more carbohydrates than you burn up every day, your body stores them as fat for use at a later time.

PROTEIN

Every single cell in our bodies needs protein to stay healthy. Our bodies need protein to help us repair cells as well as to make new ones. Meat, seafood, poultry, beans, eggs, seeds, and nuts all contain protein. People who are vegetarians don't eat meat so they need to use other foods such as nuts and beans to give them the protein they need.

Some fat in your diet is good for you. Your body needs dietary fats to give you energy and to support the growth of your cells.

Fats help you absorb the nutrients you eat into your body and help you to produce the important hormones you need for your organs to function well. Avocadoes, olive oil, and butter all contain fat.

GOOD FOOD

If you eat the right types of foods, your body will receive all the five basic types of nutrients it needs to stay healthy. Some foods have lots of nutrients and others don't.

In addition to the vitamins, minerals, carbohydrates, protein, and fat that you need, all healthy foods, except for pure drinking water, have calories. Calories are the units of energy that the food contains. You need a certain range of calories every day. If you need 2,000 calories per day and you eat 4,000 per day, you'll gain weight.

Here are some general guidelines for what you should be eating every day.

You should be eating at least 1,200 calories every day and as many as 2,000 calories daily depending on how active you are. You'll need at least 3 ounces and as much as 5.5 ounces of protein. You'll need about 2 cups of fruits and about 2.5 cups of vegetables. You'll need about 5 or 6 ounces of grains and about 2.5 cups of dairy products, such as milk and yogurt.

A HEALTHY DIET

You'll need to make good choices to keep your diet healthy.

PROTEIN

Every day you should be eating some lean protein, such as seafood, lean meat, poultry, eggs, beans, or peas. Nuts and seeds that are unsalted are good choices too. All these choices are healthy proteins.

FRUITS

You can pick any type of fruit you want—bananas, berries, apples, pears—are just a few examples. Citrus fruits, like oranges and grapefruit, are good for you too. There are so many delicious fruits and they have natural sugars to keep your "sweet tooth" happy. You can have fruit juice too. Just be sure that it's 100% juice and doesn't have added sugar.

VEGETABLES

Some people don't like vegetables, but when they're prepared properly they're delicious! Asparagus, broccoli, spinach, carrots, bell peppers, and arugula are just a few types of the different flavorful vegetables you can choose for a healthy diet.

GRAINS

Choose whole grains like whole-wheat bread or brown rice. Oatmeal, quinoa, and popcorn are healthy too. Just be careful not to put too much butter or salt on your popcorn. Try to limit the amount of white flour you eat. It's not as healthy as whole grains because it doesn't have much fiber.

DAIRY

Drink fat-free or low-fat milk and eat yogurt, cheese, or drinks that contain fortified soy to get your daily needs for dairy.

It's pretty easy to eat healthy if you're aware of the types of foods you should be eating. Don't forget to drink plenty of pure water too!

JUNK FOOD

Junk food isn't actually made of junk or garbage. The term "junk food" means something that may taste good but is loaded with too many calories, sugar, salt, or fat based on the serving size you eat. This type of "food" isn't really food at all because it doesn't provide you with healthy nutrients.

For example, candy and sugary sodas fall in the category of junk food because they are mostly sugar with few nutrients. Cookies and chips are junk food too. In fact, if it's processed and you can take it out of a package to eat it, more than likely it's junk food.

ROTTEN FOOD

Food that's gotten rotten smells bad or has patches of mold on it. Food can get spoiled or go rotten even in the refrigerator. If it has mold, smells funny, or tastes strange, don't eat it. Just throw it out. The other way that food can be harmful is if it hasn't been cooked to a high enough temperature. Many raw foods have harmful bacteria that can make you sick if the food isn't cooked at a high enough internal temperature.

EAT SMART!

In order to eat healthy and get the nutrients you need for energy, you need to eat the right foods and the right number of calories each day. When you choose the right amounts from the food groups of fruits, vegetables, proteins, grains, and dairy, you'll be getting the vitamins, minerals, proteins, carbohydrates, and fats you need. You'll also need to keep the right balance of carbohydrates and calories so you don't gain weight. Stay away from junk food if you want to stay healthy and never eat food that's spoiled!

Awesome! Now that you know more about the types of foods that are good for you and the types of foods that aren't, you may want to find out more about the different Food Groups in the Baby Professor book The Food Groups – Nutrition Books for Kids.

Visit
BABY PROFESSOR
EDUCATION KIDS
www.BabyProfessorBooks.com
to download Free Baby Professor eBooks
and view our catalog of new and exciting
Children's Books